READING ABOUT

My Family

By Jim Pipe

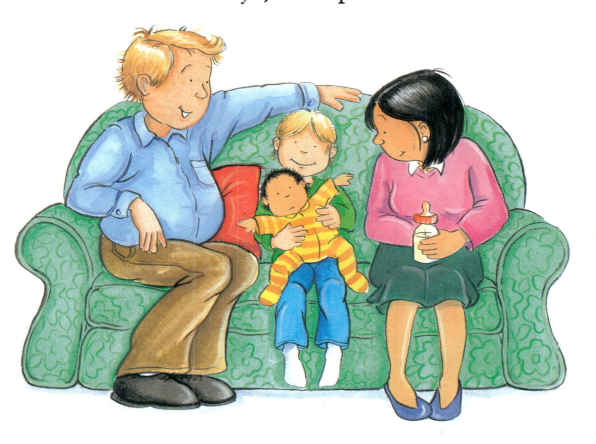

Aladdin/Watts
London • Sydney

Family pictures

2

Hi! I am Anthony.

I am making a family tree. This shows everyone in my family.

Would you like to meet them?

Making a
family tree

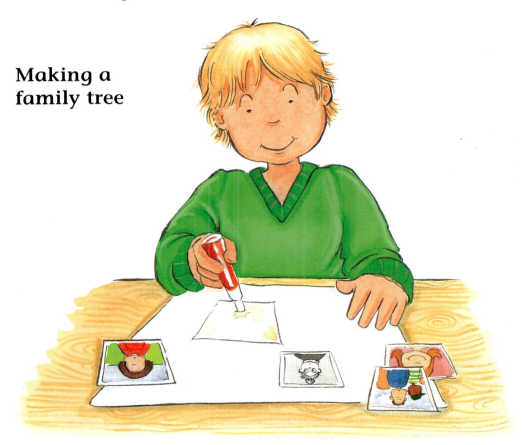

This is my mother.

Her name is Angela, but I call her Mum. Here she is making a cake.

Making
a cake

Mum used to be a dancer.

Now she runs classes at the gym.

At the gym

This is my father.

His name is Roger, but most people call him Spike. I call him Dad.

He drives a big digger and helps to build the roads.

Dad

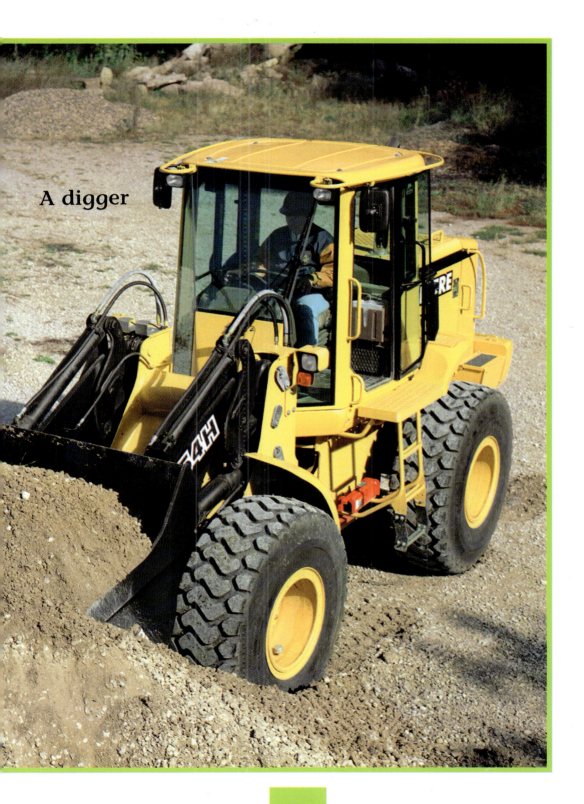

A digger

Meet my sister Karen.

She is twelve and plays the flute in the school band.

School band

Sometimes she helps me with my homework.

Doing my homework

But sometimes my sister can be very bossy.

This is my baby brother Tim.
He is only three.

He is still learning to talk,
so he calls me "Ant".

Baby
brother

I like playing with him sometimes.

But when my friends are here,
I want him to go away.

Playing
with friends

I have four grandparents.
Here are Dad's mum and dad.

When I visit them, Grandpa
takes me fishing.
Grandma
likes to go
swimming.

Grandparents

12

Fishing

Uncle Frank is Mum's brother.

He drives a fast red car and likes to honk its horn.

Mum says he is very silly.

Fast car

But when Uncle Frank makes silly faces, we all laugh.

He can also do great magic tricks.

Doing a magic trick

Uncle Matt is my Dad's brother.

He is a fire fighter. He wears a special suit with a yellow helmet.

Fire fighter

Aunt Marie is his wife. Their baby is called Ricky.

Ricky is my cousin. He does not do much, but he makes lots of noise.

My uncle

My cousin and I

My aunt

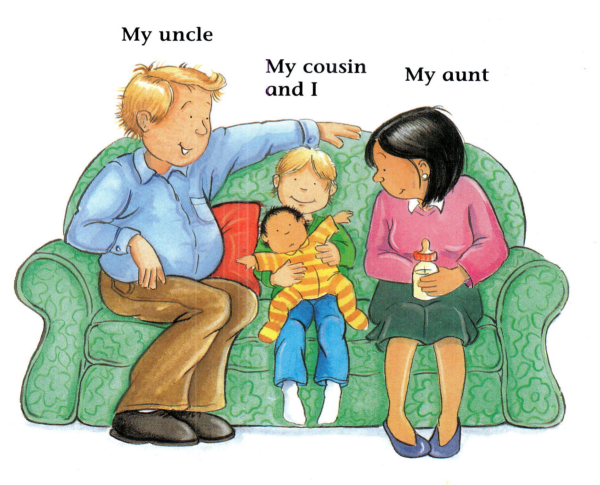

Guess what!

Today is my birthday and everyone has come for my party.

Look at all my presents!

Presents

Can you guess which present
Uncle Matt gave me?

Here is my family tree.

All my grandparents are at the top.

My parents, aunt and uncles are in the middle.

At the bottom are my cousin, my brother, my sister…

…and ME, Anthony!

Family tree

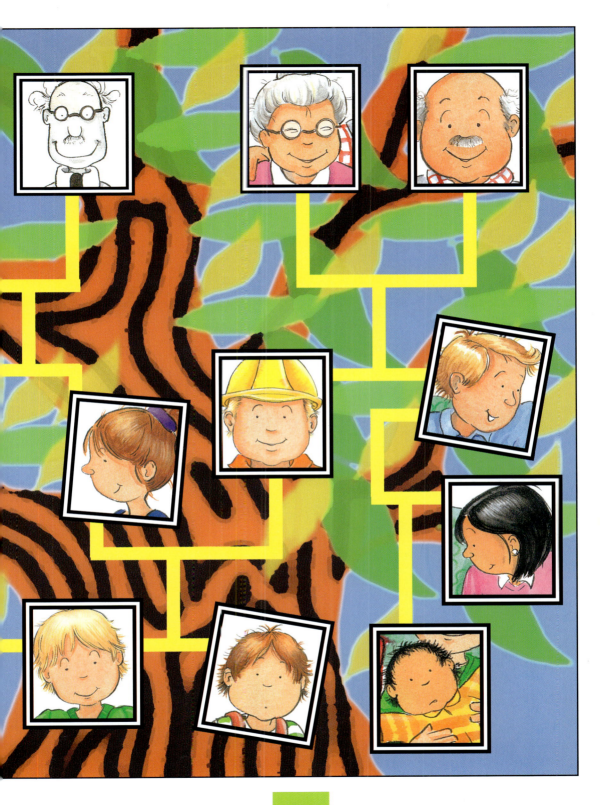

Here are some words and phrases from the book.

Grandparents

Make a family tree

Cousin

Drive a car

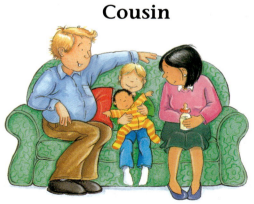

Aunt and uncle

At the gym

Play with friends

Sister

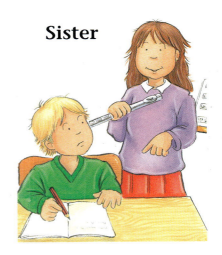

Go fishing

Do homework

Can you use these words to write your own story?

Did you see these in the book?

Lamp

Teddy bear

Hose

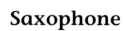

Saxophone

© Aladdin Books Ltd 2001
All rights reserved
Designed and produced by
Aladdin Books Ltd
28 Percy Street
London W1T 2BZ
Literacy Consultant
Ann Hawken
Printed in U.A.E.

ISBN 0 7496 4841 4
First published in
Great Britain in 2001 by
Franklin Watts
96 Leonard Street
London EC2A 4XD
A catalogue record for this
book is available from the
British Library.

Illustrator Mary Lonsdale - SGA
Picture Credits
All photos by Select Pictures
except 5, 23tr – Steve
Chenn/CORBIS; 7 – John
Deere; 8, 24br – Bob Rowan:
Progressive Image/CORBIS;
13, 23ml – Bob Winsett/
CORBIS; 16, 24bl – Scania.